Set Plan Commit

Accomplish Your Ultimate Happiness Goals

Tadas Bite

BALBOA.
PRESS
A DIVISION OF HAY HOUSE

Balboa Press books may be ordered through booksellers or by contacting:

Balboa Press
A Division of Hay House
1663 Liberty Drive
Bloomington, IN 47403
www.balboapress.com
1 (877) 407-4847

Because of the dynamic nature of the Internet, any web addresses or links contained in this book may have changed since publication and may no longer be valid. The views expressed in this work are solely those of the author and do not necessarily reflect the views of the publisher, and the publisher hereby disclaims any responsibility for them.

The author of this book does not dispense medical advice or prescribe the use of any technique as a form of treatment for physical, emotional, or medical problems without the advice of a physician, either directly or indirectly. The intent of the author is only to offer information of a general nature to help you in your quest for emotional and spiritual well-being. In the event you use any of the information in this book for yourself, which is your constitutional right, the author and the publisher assume no responsibility for your actions.

This book is a work of non-fiction. Unless otherwise noted, the author and the publisher make no explicit guarantees as to the accuracy of the information contained in this book and in some cases, names of people and places have been altered to protect their privacy.

Any people depicted in stock imagery provided by Thinkstock are models, and such images are being used for illustrative purposes only.
Certain stock imagery © Thinkstock.

Print information available on the last page.

ISBN: 978-1-5043-8583-1 (sc)
ISBN: 978-1-5043-8585-5 (hc)
ISBN: 978-1-5043-8584-8 (e)

Library of Congress Control Number: 2017912292

Balboa Press rev. date: 08/08/2017

ACKNOWLEDGEMENT

This book has been a product of happiness found in my life. I found happiness because of my wife Colleen Bite. She has helped me discover Ultimate Happiness and because of her, this book exists today. Thank you Colleen for all of your support, editing, and your ideas to make this goal come true. Thank you to my family Andrius, Alison, and Anjel for reading the first proof of this book. Receiving feedback really added value to the content. I have been talking about this book for three years and it's finally here, I want to express how grateful I am for the friends and family in my life who helped and encouraged me to continue and finish this goal. I also want to say thank you to Balboa Press for working really hard to make this book come true. Without all of your support this couldn't be possible. Thank you everyone for all of your help ☺

Thank you Mom and Dad for raising me and always believing in me ☺

TABLE OF CONTENTS

PLAN

Commit

ABOUT THE AUTHOR

Tadas Bite is a first-generation Lithuanian. His parents brought him to the U.S. at the age of eleven. He was a kid who had to learn the English language and make new friends. He lived a normal life struggling in school and mostly being the class clown. He will be the first one to tell you that he has made more mistakes in his life than he can count. He has lived an interesting life thus far and he wants to share with you how he changed and what made him change for the better. He's not perfect but he has embraced many positive traits. Tadas wasn't always a positive person and a multitasking superstar as some of his friends have referred to him. He was just an average person with many various obstacles in the way of achieving success at being happy. Despite many obstacles he obtained his Bachelor's degree in Industrial Engineering and earned his Master's in Technology from Purdue University while working various odd jobs to pay for school and enjoying his hobby of bodybuilding. Currently he is working as an Engineer for a major medical device manufacturing company. At the same time, he is pursuing his dream to retire from his current profession and continue to work on the one true passion he has. Tadas wants to help the world become a happier place to live for everyone. His transformation started with setting goals and accomplishing them. Soon after he accomplished some of his goals his life transformed into something he has never dreamed of before. He has overcome many obstacles and worked very hard to get where he is now. He is so happy with the way his life has turned out and he is literally living in a happy dream now. He is so excited about sharing his story with you and how we can change to overcome anything and accomplish everything. He simply set goals, and accomplishes them and he wants to show you how, so you can end up being ultimately happy.

Tadas mission in life is to help everyone in the world become happier.

He wrote this book to show each reader how easy it really is to set your goals for ultimate happiness and achieve them.

INTRODUCTION

There are many obstacles that life throws our way and many more challenges that we must face every day which hinder our ability to set goals, plan, and actually accomplish them. This book is for someone who wants to find out what they really want out of life. It is here to provide helpful information that will assist everyone in accomplishing all of their goals. This is for people who want to lose weight, gain weight, get out of debt, become a doctor, get a promotion, buy a house, pay off a car loan, quit a bad habit, become employee of the year, find your purpose in life, become happier, or anything in life that requires planning, motivation, and execution. This book applies to anyone who has a goal and if you don't have one yet, this book will help you set new goals and accomplish them. It is written by me to show everyone who reads this book how simple everything can be, even if you have challenges along the way. You can accomplish anything you want if you plan, prepare for the future, have a positive attitude, and persevere. If you think that life is hard this book is for you.

How does this book work?

The book is set up with 3 sections, Set, Plan, and Commit. The first section will help you find yourself and help you understand what you really want. Read this section to understand your true needs. This section will help you set the right goas for yourself to achieve ultimate happiness. Section two is about planning your goals. This section will help you understand what you need to do to plan properly. It will go over learning how to plan and why planning is so important. In the last section you will commit to your plans. This section will help you find your motivation and helpful tips to make your life better when achieving your goals. Have an open mind and follow the exercises, which will help set your ultimate happiness goals and prepare you to achieve them. Now that you understand how this book works, read it!

SET

Planning a goal may seem simple for many of us. We decide what our goal is and we try to reach it without any thought about it. Many of us set a date to lose 10 pounds and hit the gym as hard as we can to lose the weight. After that date has passed and we have not seen any results we give up and forget what the goal was. Then there are people who set goals that are important to them and they do anything possible to successfully achieve them.

This leads us to the first section of the book that is entitled SET. This section is all about setting your goals but before we can set the goals we must know who we really are, why we want something, and what the right goals are for us. Many of us do not set the correct goals and that is the reason for not following through with them. There are many ways we can set goals and ensure we reach them. We will explore what it really takes to set the proper goal. We will learn who we are, what influences we have, what we really want, and set the goals which will lead us to ultimate happiness.

Section Overview

- Know Who You Are
- Influences
- How to be you
- Want and Fail or Need and Succeed
- Set Your Goals
- Reflect On Your Goal

CHAPTER 1

KNOW WHO YOU ARE

"Knowing yourself is the beginning
of all wisdom." Aristotle

One of the most difficult tasks in life can be finding ourselves and what we want. The reason behind that is simple, there are many influences in life such as television, celebrities, friends, and family that usually shape us into who we are. We can't seem to find ourselves within ourselves and sometimes we do things for others. This creates a problem for all of us and the goals we set out for ourselves are not necessarily what we want, they do not work, or we just don't put the effort in them the way we should.

Finding myself was a lengthy journey, I was influenced by everything around me from actors on TV to friends and family every day in my life. Up until I turned twenty-five I was still confused as to who I really was. I was constantly trying to impress my friends and peers and worried about what everyone else thought of me. Currently I have been able to do what I want to do on my own terms. I have found out who I want to be and I don't particularly worry about what anyone else thinks as long as I'm happy and it doesn't hurt anyone else. This includes how I live, what I eat, what music I listen to, how I spend my money, and many other miscellaneous things.

I remember starting college. It was a time in my life right after earning my High School Diploma. The goal was simple "Graduate" little did I know the goal came from my peers and it was the wrong goal. I decided to go to school because everyone else thought it was a good idea for me. I didn't know what I wanted to do and I wasn't sure what to go to school for. I enrolled and started taking the basic courses and by the third semester I dropped out because I just wasn't feeling it and I did not know where I would end up if I continued going.

There was another time in my life when I decided to become a Realtor shortly after I stopped going to college. I received my Real Estate license and I was ready to sell some houses. This little idea to become a Realtor came from my mom. She thought it would be something I would like to do so I did it. I sold a few homes and saved up a few hundred dollars. I didn't enjoy being a realtor and decided to leave the business after only seven months of being a part of it. So, this idea didn't work out and being a realtor was not a good choice for me. As you can see the decision was not my own and I did it because it made my mom happy to see that I was trying to do something with my life. At the same time near the end of my Real Estate career I had approximately two thousand dollars and some credit left on my credit cards. I always wanted to live in California so I packed up and drove there. It was a roller-coaster ride but one thing is certain that I finally decided what I wanted to do with my life after living there for a few years.

Once I got to California I started working at a home improvement store, I climbed the ranks in less than one year and became a department manager. I worked hard and put in the overtime to be the best employee possible. Once I achieved this I realized my limited options and the time it would take to move up even more. After two years as a department manager I decided to go back to school and complete what I started. Remember I had some courses complete and now it was time to go back to school. I worked out a deal with my management team and it looked promising to go to school. Half way through the semester my management told me I had to have open availability and I could not get certain days off to continue going to school. I felt bad and I dropped my classes. I also made up my mind about what I really wanted to do in life so I set the goal of graduating from college. This goal was more complicated I wanted an engineering degree and because I love making things better I researched Industrial Engineering. This was my own goal and I was able to commit and dedicate the next 4 years of my life to it. I will explain in detail what made me choose this goal and why I pursued it with passion in the "Plan" section when I talk about learning.

I moved back home to live with my parents and enrolled in Purdue University Calumet. It was very affordable with in-state tuition. I started working a job with set hours at a tire distribution center where I loaded and unloaded around eighty thousand pounds of tires by hand five days a week to earn the money and pay for school. So, please let me explain how difficult this was, I had to load two to three semitrailers full of tires in an interlocking pattern up to the ceiling by hand in about eight hours. The job was the most physically exhausting work I have ever done. I also want to add the temperature in the Chicago land area, it wasn't great either, freezing cold in the winter or steaming hot in the summer. This is also inside of a dark and dirty fifty-three foot trailer. In a few words to sum it up, I hated this job. I worked hard so I could continue to work towards a very specific goal that came from within. This working situation was the most motivating for me at the time to continue towards my goal so I can get out of working there.

Simple Exercise

Take some time to think of recent goals you set out for yourself really think of who created those goals especially the ones you have not been able to achieve.

Write down your goals, where the idea came from, and if you failed or succeeded.

My Example:

Go to College came from peers the first time: Failed

Become a Realtor came from family: Failed

Go to College and receive an Industrial Engineering Degree came from within: Successful

This was just a small sample of my goals. You can see the trend, if the goals are not your own you will be less likely to successfully complete them.

This exercise is here to help you understand why some of your goals in the past have not been successful. Hopefully you realized that some of the goals you have not met were from someone else and not your own beliefs. Now that you know the reason why you didn't succeed before you can be more confident at setting new goals. This exercise should help you with a confidence boost and motivate you to set new goals.

Influences

There are many influences in our lives. Everywhere we turn someone is telling you what to do and they all try to provide life advice. Many times you hear someone say something like… well I been married 20 years and, "we are happy because we never went to bed angry and you should do this if you want to stay happy..." and another person has another opinion of what makes a marriage work. Maybe you will find yourself talking to a mechanic and they are telling you things that they know. Usually they tell you that you should do what they did because that is the only way it works. As you can see many people have their own opinions and while it may be great advice it may not be the best advice for you.

If you want to be yourself, you must do what you want to do. If you like what you hear or it is something you would do then by all means do it but if it's not, don't change yourself. If someone tells you that this is the only way to do something, it may not be the case. There is almost never one single way to do a specific thing especially when you are talking about life.

How to be you

It's easy to be yourself, all you have to do is be yourself. Imagine when you are alone at home and you can do whatever you want without anyone judging you. This is the time when you are 100% yourself. You can play video games, listen to any genre of music, watch movies, eat whatever and no one will judge you. So if you really want to learn how to be yourself do what you would when you are alone and carless of what others are thinking. This will help you become more comfortable with yourself and if you practice this when you are with others you may just become yourself around others too.

There are many ways you can imagine being alone and pretending that no one is watching but this is not about hiding, this is about becoming who you truly are. Stop making everyone else happy just because they are there now, in the end it's your own happiness that will make you feel good. When it comes to relationships it's different but it should be 50/50 because no two people are the same and everyone likes different things. So if you were yourself and met the person of your dreams then it should be easy to share the common things.

Being yourself is a matter of not being afraid to be judged by anyone else. This is a fear that all of us have only so we can fit in with the rest of the population. It's scary to think of being an outsider but it can be much more rewarding when everyone starts respecting you more because you're not afraid to show them who you truly are.

CHAPTER 2

WANT AND FAIL OR NEED AND SUCCEED

"The world as we have created it is a process of our thinking. It cannot be changed without changing our thinking." Albert Einstein

The best part of setting goals is that it is up to you to decide what you need and what the goals can be. No one in this world can ever tell you that your goal is wrong or it will never happen. Goals appear to be easy to set all you have to do is follow your dreams and make sure that they are as you need them to be but it's not that easy and you have to ensure you know how to set them properly.

How do you really know what you want? We tend to just think of the things that we want and list them out on a sheet of paper. This is the wrong approach to goal setting, so please do not just list your wants. Before you start thinking of what you really want you have to block out all the things that you think you want... let's say you saw that add for a brand new car and an attractive couple was driving it. Do you really want the car or do you want to be that couple? Advertising is developed for us to want to buy things and just because you saw it on TV or Internet it doesn't mean you want it. It could be some other aspect that you want and think that you will have if you get what the advertisement is showing. It is very interesting how our brain works when we hear and see things, we get influenced by the opposite sex or same sex whatever it may be but if you step back and take a look at what we really need, it is the only things we should want. Why does someone buy a million dollar car when they don't need it, one that is thirty thousand would provide the same transportation means. We are all influenced by advertising, celebrities, and friends. Life is about you and what you need.

When setting goals do not make the same mistakes most of us have. When setting a goal the biggest mistake is telling yourself you want something. Wanting something doesn't set you up to have the correct mindset, it simply sets you up to dream while lacking the actions to achieve it. I want to own an island or an exotic car, those goals are very enjoyable to say out loud but they have no meaning in your brain. Needing something is just a better way to set the goals and make them a reality. This is true for everyone, if you need it, you will do much more in your power to achieve it. If you just want it, your goals can always wait until tomorrow and never come true. So now go ahead and need it, make those goals come true because there is nothing that is stopping you from doing so. You can start working towards your needs today.

Now that we know why some of the goals we set are not for us, why goals fail, and the type of goals we can set, let's reflect on the things that mean the most to us. We have to think of the things we need most and what makes us happy.

Simple Exercise

Take some time to think of what you need and write it down. This will give you a great start on setting your goals. Well this is a tricky request most human needs are food, shelter, and the means of getting those two things like a job or money. So go ahead and write down your needs but then add a few Items that you need to make your life better in all of those aspects.

Write down your needs.

My Example:

I need a place to live.

I need food to survive.

I need a job.

I need transportation.

I need love from my family.

I need to spend more time with my family.

I need to live a fulfilling life which gives more meaning to life other than just surviving.

I need to help others achieve their goals and have happy lives.

I need to share my life experience.

After you set the needs I hope you understand that your needs are different from your wants. When you decide that you need something, you can't live without it, you will focus on achieving it, and you will need to have it because you need it. A want is something you can live without and you don't need to have it so you won't pursue it with as much passion. Hopefully this exercise helped you put the need in your mind and you will pursue that need with everything you have in your power to attain it.

CHAPTER 3

SET YOUR GOALS

"A goal properly set is halfway reached." Zig Ziglar

Up to this point we have found out who we are, what influences we have, how to be ourselves, and what our needs are. We have come a long way already. Now we move to the hardest part, which is making the decisions to set the right goal. Previous exercise helped us understand our needs to help with our goal setting in this chapter.

Before we move on to actual goal setting lets understand what type of goals there are. There are goals that may seem overwhelming and discourage you from attempting them. There are some goals that take years to accomplish such as receiving a degree from a University, it usually takes a minimum of 4 years. This may seem like a long time for many of us and it is. There are multiple other things that can take years such as getting to your goal weight whether it's losing or gaining it. Some things can only take a few hours such as running a marathon but training can go on for month's even years for some. Other things can take minutes such as holding your breath under water for an extended period of time. Setting goals is the easy part considering how long it takes to achieve it. The path that follows to achieving your goals may take time to accomplish. You have to practice goal setting and then taking the steps to reach those goals. Start out by setting small goals and build up to reaching your ultimate goal. I have set many small goals that eventually became habits which I do every day. I set goals to wake up at the same time at 4:30AM without pressing the snooze button, now it's automatic, most days I wake up before the alarm goes off. Another goal I set was to go to the gym before work every day which is now a habit. No human was born capable of doing anything, we all had to set goals and then learn everything we do today.

All of us are very capable of doing anything we desire. All it takes to accomplish anything is setting the right goals. We have to set the goals with the right intentions, the correct way, and for the right purpose. Set your goal with the mindset that nothing will stop you in accomplishing it. You have to believe that you need this goal to survive and it will prepare you mentally to do what it takes to achieve it.

Simple Exercise

Review your needs in the previous exercise and think of one thing that you need which can make all your needs much better and make you happy if you accomplish it.

Write down what you need and what the goal is. Remember to think of it as something you will be able to achieve. You can use any goal setting principle you choose or you can also use the Specific, Measurable, Achievable, Relevant, and Time bound (SMART) goal principle. There are many goal setting principles out there if you google them you can choose the one you prefer.

Write down your needs.

My Example:

I need to make this world a happier place for everyone by becoming a globally recognized motivational speaker on the subject of happiness and how to become successful at being happy.

I will have 500 million followers on social media globally who will help spread positivity in the world.

I will achieve my goal by July 23rd, 2020.

Reflect on Your Goal

Now that you have found out what you need, how does it make you feel to think of the things that you are imagining? It must feel good to think about your dream or how your life could be if you only had this one thing in your life or that one goal accomplished.

Take what you written down or pictures of how you imagine what you have written down and post it in your house, somewhere that you can see it all the time. Find places where you always look and post it there. Post it on your mirror so every morning you can remind yourself what you are working towards. This will help you remember and also inspire you to work towards that goal because it will be in your face every day.

Currently as I'm finishing this Chapter I have this book laying on my table. I have printed a few pages and left it there so I can look at the cover page every morning and think of something to add to it. Leaving this book laying around reminds me of the goal I set out to reach and soon it will be complete. To become more motivated and to keep pursuing my goal I keep telling myself how easy it is to write this book just to help me stay motivated to finish by this date 30 July, 2017 ☺

PLAN

Now that you had the opportunity to learn how to set the proper goal. This section will help you understand what it takes to reach the goal. The most important part of the goal you just set is the framework of how you will accomplish it. This section will prepare you for planning and how you will complete your goals. Topics to be covered in this section will include planning and learning new things.

Section Overview

- Plan for Success

- Get It Done!

- Learn

- Why Learn?

- How Do You Learn?

- Plan That Goal

CHAPTER 4

PLAN FOR SUCCESS

"A goal without a plan is just a wish."

Antoine de Saint-Exupéry

Be a dreamer and then plan to accomplish your dreams. Many fail to plan and the dreams never come true but here is the secret for success and it's planning every dream you have and believing that you will accomplish it. Planning is the key for success. There are some people that accomplish everything without planning but that's only when someone wins the lotto and it does not happen too often. Even to win the lotto you actually have to plan to get the lottery ticket so there it goes planning is the key to success.

Successfully planning is something that has to accompany every goal you set up and there has to be many details in your plan. Planning is easy just research what it takes to get something and then plan around what you know. If you want to open your own business research the business and how to start one, there may also be a business plan involved and many financial details. Sounds easy enough all you have to do is follow the steps that you found in your research that you have conducted. Planning could also involve how to make a million dollars if that is your goal. I have read many books about happiness and joy, so I'm taking the tips and advice from those who have done the same but I'm coming up with my own ideas to reach my goals. My goals don't involve making millions, I'm just planning how to make a change in this world for the better, sustain happiness in my life, and those who surround me. Mostly what we want to plan for, someone out there has already done the same and the best part is that they usually write a book or some other documentary that reveals how they did it. Take the plans that you have read about and make them your own.

I have found planning to be a great advantage for me. By organizing my schedule, planning my days and times when I do the things that need to get done without procrastinating, I am able to accomplish many goals all at once. I was working full time, working toward a personal best fitness goal, going to graduate school full time and writing this book. This is just a small sample of what I mean by planning and having more time to do everything you want.

As long as you plan and keep to your schedule you can accomplish everything you ever wanted. Planning is the key to success and it helps you accomplish all of your goals. Many of us fail to plan and have a difficult time achieving our goals. Remember that if you plan you will succeed but of course planning is just the beginning.

Get It Done!

Once you have set the goal and planned everything out the fun begins and that is actually doing what you have to do to get it done. There is no room for excuses or complaints for each and every obstacle that comes your way, it's part of life so deal with it and get it done right away.

We all have a time in our day when we are the most productive. When I was going for my undergraduate the best time for me to be productive was on Friday night. I wasn't sure why but I was able to focus on my work just sit there in my room and complete all of my course work.

It was a good time for me to focus but as time went on and things have been changing the best time for me during graduate school and currently is in the morning on Saturday and Sunday. Since I'm used to getting up early, I get up early and work on something. Currently I'm editing this book at 4:30AM on a Saturday. I just want to share this with you and show you that you can find time to do what you want and even more. You just have to find your own most productive time.

CHAPTER 5

LEARN

"Live as if you were to die tomorrow. Learn as if you were to live forever." Mahatma Gandhi

Ever wonder how important learning is? Well it's the most important thing we do in our lives. We have learned something new everyday day since we were born. Things like learning how to speak and walk. We also learned how to add and multiply numbers. We have learned how to ride a bicycle and drive a car. We have gone to school, learned history and science. We have learned to fly to space and operate on other people. We have cured many diseases and invented multiple things to make life easier. When you think about how much we have learned as a society and how advanced we are now it's incredible to see how much further we will go. We are all capable of anything extraordinary. All of us have one thing in common, we have a brain that is capable of anything. We have to use this brain to do extraordinary things. Never stop learning, never give up, and keep trying to learn more every day.

I was sixteen when I worked on an old car with my father and the words "It's easy, let's do it now!" came out of my mouth and my father started to yell that replacing an engine in a car is not easy at all! I was confused when he said that it's not easy to replace an engine in a car and he started to explain every little detail about what it involves to replace an engine in the car. After all of the details he told me, I told him "it is easy you already know every detail of replacing this engine" and after a few hours we were done replacing the engine. The engine replacement would have taken even less time if I didn't keep telling my father how easy everything was and then he had to stop and explain why it's not easy as he was doing what he was doing to remove and replace the engine. This is a warning, it's not easy to replace an engine in a car but the idea of it being easy makes it less difficult and it puts a positive spin on replacing the car's engine. Also this statement can be used for any task "It's easy". It's much easier to do something when you keep telling yourself it's easy instead of its impossible. It's like an incantation where you keep telling yourself something over and over again. A good example is when someone asks you to find something but you keep telling yourself I don't know where it is over and over again and you can't see it even when it's right in your hand. I think this happens to many of us. I was looking for my phone

one day and kept telling my wife I can't find my phone anywhere, this lasted for 5 minutes. Guess where I found the phone? The phone was in my hand the whole time. So the point I'm trying to make here is that if you keep telling yourself it's easy over and over again you may start believing it and complete anything you ever wanted because "it's so easy."

Many of the things we learn and use repeatedly we become great at. It is very simple to learn even the most complicated task if you divide the task in to simple steps. Many people go to a Department Store and buy furniture, most have never attempted to build furniture before and yet they buy it and assemble it mostly without any problems. This is true because all of the furniture comes with simple instructions that tell you where to put the screws and bolts and then assemble the pieces. If you don't have the instructions it is almost impossible to assemble that furniture but with instructions it's very simple. I want to show that even difficult tasks can become very simple and easy to accomplish when they are broken down in to simple steps. This is just an example but it can be applied to anything.

When we take a look at the replacement of an engine in a car it can be simple. If you own a repair manual or know someone who is knowledgeable of the process it will become easy to replace the engine. There may be more steps than required for furniture but the process is the same and this idea can be applied to many other things. In school there are classes we have to take and our course guide tells us what to take to complete the degree. Then in class we receive a syllabus which tells us what we need to do to pass the class. We also receive a book which tells us all the information we need to know to complete the assignments and pass the tests. All there is to do is follow the simple steps one at a time and successfully complete them until we reach our goals.

The same idea can be used for weight loss, weight gain, becoming anything you want professionally, opening a business, writing a book, ..., and anything else that requires following directions or doing what needs to be done to accomplish any task.

I wanted to learn how to ride a motorcycle so I could buy one and check of one of the goals on my list. One way to learn is to ask someone who rides and listen to them and take notes on the basics. Another way is to go online and watch a video on how to do it or find a book about riding motorcycles. The last step is to jump on that motorcycle with protective gear in an empty parking lot and attempt what you have learned. I watched a video, read about it online and bought a bike. I practiced in the parking lot for about one hour and then I was able to ride home. After following those steps you can learn how to ride a motorcycle. The hardest part of riding the motorcycle was the fear I had to get over. I was afraid to ride, then mess something up, and fall over. All those thoughts that run through your head when attempting something new, well I had all of them and my life felt like it was in danger. It's pretty extreme to think of dying when getting on a motorcycle but I had that run through my head. I eventually convinced myself that I wanted to do this since I was a kid and this is my chance to learn. Hey I already bought the bike. I choose to ride the motorcycle and get over my fear.

Why Learn?

There are many reasons that I can state here and explain the benefits of learning new things. I will tell you a story instead of a time in my life where I was stuck in a rut and didn't know how to get out of it. When I lived in California and started working in a hardware store I put in a great amount of effort to move up from a Sales Associate to Sales Specialist and then to a Department

Manager. It was quite a challenge to move up three positions in one year but I did it and I felt that I have accomplished something. I was making $42,000 a year and I made enough money to live with a roommate. After the second year I started questioning myself about the future and what I can accomplish. After thinking about it I decided to do some research and ask many questions.

I questioned everyone I worked with about their experiences working at this place and what the future holds for all of us. I found out that if I took an upper management position I would actually make less money than I did at the time and have to work 60 hour work weeks. Everyone kept telling me that to move up sometimes you have to take a pay cut and that sounded ludicrous to me. There is no way I would take a pay cut and work more hours to make less money, who can imagine that?

The decision I made after I learned the truth at this hardware store was very difficult. I had to debate and research what is the best outcome for me in the future. My choices were to keep working paycheck to paycheck in California dealing with roommate issues or move back home to Indiana and go to school, so I could eventually make more money doing something I love and live comfortable. The decision was not easy, I had many credit card bills, and a decision to move back home after you have moved out isn't simple. Learning about the options I had and after further investigation of what I needed to do I decided to move back home and go to school.

This decision that I made was very difficult but the reason that I made it was because I researched and learned about the future and what it held for me in the current state that I was in. By learning I was able to make the most educated guesses as to the outcome of my decisions. Learning helped me understand how to make the best decisions in life. If we do not learn anything new from the day we graduate high school we will not be able to advance further in life and get stuck in a rut the way I was.

Now as I am writing this chapter I have already graduated with my Master's Degree and I'm writing this book to help people understand that anything is possible. Trust me when I say this that I never want to look back and think of where I would be if I didn't go back to school. I am very happy with the decision I made and it's due to me learning more about my previous job.

How Do You Learn?

Learning is fun! It can be even more fun when you figure things out on your own. Many people ask questions and receive advice from others how to do something.

Many times that is sufficient and the best thing is that when you are learning there is no such thing as a dumb question so don't be afraid to ask as many questions as you want. We can learn anything we want and all of us are capable of it. We can learn how to drive cars we can even learn how to fly a plane. Everything we learned so far was difficult in the beginning but now it's simple and easy. When you think about it we have learned the English language and some of us know multiple languages. We are capable of learning almost anything in the world as long as we actually want to do it for ourselves.

There are many resources available to us so we can learn about anything we want. The most convenient technology to research and learn about new things is the internet if used properly. One of the best places to learn is your public library.

The internet search engine is the most convenient and the best tool to do preliminary research about something you want to learn about. By using multiple search engines you will be able to find different sources for the same information if it's widely available. Using the internet you have to be very careful and verify all of the sources sometimes internet sources may not be accurate so it is best if the sources are from published books or peer reviewed journals.

The best source for learning just about anything is the library where many books, journals, dictionaries, and encyclopedias are in abundance. Journals usually have more recent data and statistics while books that have been around for a while are a little outdated but they do offer great historical data or information.

After you have gathered the information on a subject you want to pursue, read it and learn it. If you want to become a doctor read about what it takes to be a doctor, be warned there maybe multiple manuals and instructions to follow but anyone can do it eventually. If you want to learn how to write software for your computer there are multiple manuals that teach you how to do it step by step. If you want to lose weight there are many books out there. If you want to learn anything you can, but some things may take practice or just a long time to complete. No one can start a business and become a success in one day but if you do the right research, prepare, execute, and stay positive anything can be done. It's that easy too!

Plan That Goal

In this section you were provided with simple information how to learn new things and why it will help you. Now that you understand you can learn anything, use this skill to learn how to properly plan the goal you want to accomplish. Below is the simple exercise please complete this exercise before moving on to ensure you are on the right track.

Simple Exercise

Take the goal from section one and write it down. Then research this goal and review what it takes to get it done. If other people have done it, research those people. If there are guides review many of them and pick out what you like. There is almost never only one single way to accomplish any task. Please choose the right plan that suits your needs and write it down here.

Write down your plan.

My Example:

I need to make this world a happier place for everyone by becoming a globally recognized motivational speaker on the subject of happiness and how to become successful at being happy.

I will have 500 million followers on social media globally who will help spread positivity in the world.

I will achieve my goal by July 23rd, 2020.

The Plan

- Find a Mentor to help become a motivational speaker (Due 6-30-2017)
- Design a professional Website (Due 6-30-2017)
- Build an online audience on Twitter, Instagram, Facebook and Linkedin (Goal is to update content 3 times per week)
- Publish my completed book (Due 8-23-2017)
- First Successfully Happy Workshop (Due 10-7-2017)

COMMIT

Commitment, obligation, persistence, determination are some of the words that should describe you when you have set a goal and you are successfully achieving it. The easiest thing for people to do when things become difficult is to quit. The people that give up never accomplish anything. The people that never attempt anything never accomplish anything either. Remember you have to commit and complete to achieve anything. There are many ways to get motivated and this is the section that will explore the benefits of being positive and how to commit to achieving any goal you set.

Section Overview

- Find Your Motivation
- Goal Motivation
- Reward System
- Be Positive
- What is a positive attitude?
- Benefits of being positive
- Wake up feeling great every morning
- Procrastination
- Do It Now!
- Save time
- Little Changes Big Difference
- Challenge Everything
- Improve
- Be creative
- Learn to be creative

CHAPTER 6

FIND YOUR MOTIVATION

"Never, never, never give up." Winston Churchill

Getting what you want will motivate you, but if that does not help, lets read this chapter to understand what I mean. You can create vision boards or spend some time living the life that you want to live for a brief moment. You can pretend to be what you want and see if it even fits you. If everything is working out and you want this for yourself then this is when you get motivated and start working towards what you want. Visualizing and dreaming of your accomplished goals is a great way to keep motivated, to push ahead, and keep working towards where you want to be.

Goal Motivation

Tell your goals to everyone, your family, your friends, your coworkers, and people you meet every day. This will help you stay on track and actually motivate you to accomplish your goals because in the end when you run into those people again you can boast and tell them that you got it done! I tell everyone what my goals are with the hope to inspire them to set awesome goals too.

One of the most important things to do when you tell your goals to the wrong people (you know those people that have the worst life in the history of mankind and nothing good has ever happened to them) is to stop listening to them. Some people are mostly negative and if you tell them your goal is to make a million dollars this year most likely they will question you about how you will get it done and start questioning your salary or what you are doing that would make a million dollars. You don't have to describe your goals in detail just tell them about it and if they don't have anything good to say. You can tell them that being positive is going to get you half way there and the other half is doing the work like buying a lottery ticket. There you go negative person that's my plan. ☺

Don't ever give up. You set your goal and because you didn't reach it in time don't give up and stop trying, keep at it because you are probably half way there. I would be very happy to make half a million this year and try just as hard or harder to make that magic million the next year. Join a challenge any challenge, if its weight loss join a challenge and try your hardest to do everything possible to be number one. In weight loss the bigger you are the better because that change will be that much better. If you don't win the challenge, it will be OK because even if you lost a few pounds it's still way better than nothing.

Reward System

"Remember to celebrate milestones as you prepare for the road ahead." Nelson Mandela

Reward yourself and celebrate. Every task that is challenging will deserve a time that is just as rewarding and satisfying. If you completed the most challenging task of your life you deserve the most rewarding experience. If the task is to write a book and you complete it on time you can take the most extravagant trip of your life. If your goal is to work out every day and you complete it for 90 days, reward yourself with something you love. This is all up to you to decide, if you think you deserve a reward for taking out the trash do it.

The reason for the reward system is to have something that you can try to achieve. Many times we can just buy an item or treat ourselves to something nice without doing anything but that just isn't as much fun. Other times you must meet a goal and if you don't, you will never have the reward of your completed goal.

Reward yourself with every goal you meet. If you don't reward yourself after every goal you have met it will be very hard to keep setting new goals. A reward at the end of meeting your goal will encourage you to make more goals and even bigger goals that will lead to much better rewards.

I have set many goals in my life and it started when I enrolled at Purdue University. My ultimate goal was to graduate and receive my Bachelor's degree. This is a tough goal to reach and required many smaller goals for me to keep motivated and push forward to finally graduate. My smaller goals were to pass my courses and achieve a GPA of 3.5 and above. I have set smaller goals that gave me meaning at the end of every semester such as something nice like a new laptop, a trip to Florida for spring break, two trips to Hawaii, and other things if I met the goals. I had to stay with friends on my trips, since I was on a full time college student budget.

The reward system is the second most exciting part of your goal accomplishment. Reaching the goal is the most exciting but remember to enjoy the journey and the entire process from goal setting to achievement. Reaching the goal while enjoying the whole process means you will enjoy way more of your life. So enjoy the process and you will be happy.

CHAPTER 7

BE POSITIVE

"Life is 10% what happens to you and 90% how you react to it." *Charles R. Swindoll*

Being positive is something we have to learn and if you are wondering, I would like to say that there are no magical people that are born being positive. It is something we learn throughout our life and often times it's the opposite that is instilled in us because we as a society only look at the bad things. We will talk about the service we had at a restaurant that was bad instead of the one that was good. We will call a company about a product that is bad or had some minor imperfection but we will very seldom call a company and tell them how much we love something. We will talk about all of the bad news in the world but what about all of the good things that people do. I have rarely heard this statement in my life unless it came from me "the world is not getting worse, its actually better." However I have heard many versions of, "the world is getting worse and everything we hear about today is bad." When you take a look at those two statements I hope you can see that the world is probably the same if not better today than it has ever been. Thinking about medieval times and the punishments people faced sound terrible but today that doesn't happen. There are bad people that do bad things but there are many more good people that do very good things. So this is my spin on being positive and thinking about the good things.

What is a positive attitude?

Being positive is learned and it involves someone thinking with a good outlook in mind. There are people that can see many bad things but point out some good in them. Some examples that can be looked at from a positive point of view include; getting fired from a job can be terrible... but you probably didn't like it that much and you didn't perform to your fullest potential because you were not committed to it. The positive in getting fired will be that you will now have a chance to find a better job that you can enjoy and actually succeed in. Another positive from this is that it will motivate you to find the dream job, instead of going to a job you were miserable in and that drained your energy. The ending of a relationship can be terrible. The positive in this can be looked in a way where there are many fish in the sea and now you are free to find the best one! You may also think about why it ended, reflect and learn from your mistakes to ensure you don't repeat them in your new relationship. What I'm trying to say in so many words is that you can take almost any bad thing in life and put a positive spin on it.

How do you stay positive in a world that is generally filled with so much bad? Before we get to the answer we know everyone in the world does not have a positive attitude all the time. We are not born with a positive attitude but we learn either to be positive or negative. Throughout life and many unfortunate events we tend to focus on the negatives in life. However, there is a solution for learning to be positive when bad things happen. There are better more positive ways to look at any bad situation at hand. In this section we will learn how to react to different situations and put a positive spin on them.

Sometimes the world throws us bad bosses, traffic jams, finance issues, difficult school work, car trouble, and many other issues. We can either allow it to ruin our day or we can take them as a learning experience. We can deal with our issues in a positive way, like thinking about how that situation can make our lives better. Think of the bad boss at work and reflect on yourself and how you are at work. Maybe it's you and there is something you can do to make the situation better. You can also choose to think that maybe that boss will not make it another year and you can get his or her job, so step up to the plate and work harder. Traffic sucks but it's an opportunity to call your friends and catch up, it's an opportunity to listen to an audio book, and it's an opportunity to reflect on how grateful you are for all the good things in your life. Let's say you spent $70,000 on a brand new luxury car and you are feeling the financial pressure. Start to focus on the great features of the car about how nice heated leather seats will feel in the winter, the navigation that will ensure you never have to ask for directions, and how awesome the self driving feature is. These are just a few examples of thinking positive. Please try to think of something positive in a situation that you previously thought of as being negative in your life and then practice this for everything that happens in the future.

There are many times when you are happy and you feel positive all day. When you feel those happy or positive moments record them as soon as they happen and reflect on them the end of the day. This will help you understand how often you are feeling positive and what creates those moments. Learn what makes you happy, motivated, passionate, productive, and excited about life, then constantly do those things. Learn what moves you and keep doing it over and over again. I have been working out for more than twelve years now and after a really good workout I feel great. I feel a rush of happiness and energy which motivates me to do more during the day. I feel super productive all day and I'm always happy to take on new challenges. Learn what makes you happy and then keep doing those things to keep you happy.

Being positive is learned so by surrounding yourself with people who are positive will benefit you and help you become the same. The world throws many things at us that may not seem good at first but keep at it and look at the bright side of things. Do not get discouraged just keep trying. If everything in life was simple and easy everyone would have everything they wanted. The biggest obstacle in accomplishing anything is you and the fear of failure. Sometimes we give up before we had a chance to even start because of being negative. Be positive and give yourself a chance to succeed. Make friends who are positive and hang out with them. We are an average of five people we spend the most time with. Go out and make some successful positive friends and in time you will be like them.

Staying positive no matter what is a matter of thinking different and it doesn't take much effort. There will be times in your life when everything will not turn out the way you planed it. Even if you fail at something you can link it to a learning experience and just be proud that you have learned something new. Stay positive!

Benefits of being positive

There are many benefits of being positive. Being positive attracts others who are positive into your life. It surrounds you with people that can do anything and in turn help motivate you to successfully accomplish all of your goals. Being positive increases your chances of being successful. Most people like to hear good things and even when bad things are happening there should be some positive energy that will make it more bearable to get through a tough time. There are many studies that support the benefits listed here for being positive such as; live longer, be happier, be a better performer at work, school, sports, make better decisions, be more successful at your marriage, and more importantly be better at dealing with stress.

The best part of being positive. It will ensure you are in a better mood all the time.

Wake up feeling great every morning

Many of us have a tough time waking up in the morning, hitting the snooze button many times over and feeling miserable. Well most of us wake up in the morning because we have to go to work or school or another activity that we don't necessarily want to do because it's repetitive or we just hate doing those things. Well the best solution to waking up feeling great is looking forward to waking up before you go to sleep. Now let me explain, I wake up every morning at 4:30 AM and I feel great every day. I practically want to jump out of bed whether I got eight hours of sleep or only four. I want to jump out of bed because I'm excited about going to the gym. I love going to the gym and working out, it makes me feel great and energized for the rest of the day. I feel many times more productive, positive, and willing to do anything after the workout. This story is only explaining how I wake up in the morning and prepare myself but the idea here is to wake up to something you love every morning. It will be your reason for getting up and doing what you love. So, if you love cooking breakfast and you want to make the best breakfast you ever had set a date and wake up early to make it. This will make you happy and give you a reason to wake up early and look forward to the day. There are many examples if you love playing video games, wake up and play for an hour, if you love to relax and read the paper do that. The key is being creative and thinking of the things you actually want to do in the morning and do them before going to work or school. This is just a simple way to be positive, preparing for the day ahead, and actually feeling great about waking up in the morning instead of dreading your mornings. So, wake up to what you love and you will love your day ahead.

CHAPTER 8

PROCRASTINATE OR GET IT DONE

"If you want to make an easy job seem mighty hard,

just keep putting off doing it." Olin Miller

Many of us procrastinate instead of doing the things we do not want to do. When we don't want to do something we will wait until the last minute and sometimes do a terrible job just to complete the task. Many times procrastination leads to stress from the beginning to the end of the project. This causes anxiety and the fact that you have to do something you don't want to do creates negative energy. Delaying the task creates more problems and then, they compound and make it even more difficult. The alternative is to complete the task that was due right away.

Procrastination

We all have experienced procrastination whether it's completing a homework assignment, doing laundry, washing the dishes, losing weight, writing a book, or anything else that you can't imagine doing right away and want to hold off getting done. This is normal and some of us wait till the last minute to complete a task that we don't want to do. This is especially true when we don't have a deadline or anyone to hold you accountable. We come up with excuses to do other tasks that will give us an excuse to steer away and not even attempt the task that we should focus on. By the time we complete many other tasks that we really didn't even have to do we just say we ran out of time or come up with some other excuse to self-justify why we didn't do something.

There were times in my life when I used to wait until the last minute and I remember that the results were not favorable. My lessons learned were in college beginning second semester when the course work got tough. I remember finals and final papers that were assigned to me in the beginning of the semester, I procrastinated until the last week to finish them. Well, before I tell you the results of the courses I can say that I took care of all my errands before I thought of my final papers. The papers were on my mind all the time and slowed me down more than I could have imagined. I was frustrated and kept telling everyone that I have all those papers to write. I could have written the papers in the time that I spent complaining about them but I didn't know that at the time. I decided to leave four days to write four papers and study for finals at the same time. It was the toughest four days in my life that caused so much stress. I was able to write the papers and take my finals but the results were not my best. I was able to receive two A's and two B's but I could have received all A's because the courses were not that difficult. In the end I was able to do well but not my best and I spent more time complaining and stressing out about something I could have completed a very long time ago. Procrastination is not worth it. It hinders your ability to complete other tasks and also stresses you out.

Do It Now

"Do it now!" W. Clement Stone.

Getting it done is easy as long as you just do what you have to do to get it done now, do not procrastinate and do the task right away. As discussed earlier we know the effect of procrastination so why not just get to what you have to do as soon as possible. We have excuses not to do something but that should not stop any of us. I have many other tasks I could be doing besides writing this book but I set a goal and I want to see it through. I also understand that sometimes you have to walk away from something and get back to it later. This is something that is useful and will help you complete the task. If you want to finish a task after you walk away from it you have one simple rule. You have to set an exact day when you will come back to the task at hand. If you do not set a date those words that you tell yourself "I'll finish later or next week" will never come. If you tell yourself I will come back to this on such a date and schedule a time to do it, this will help you prioritize your tasks so you can accomplish it.

Save time

Saving time is about organizing your life. Being organized will save you a ton of time while doing anything. There are numerous examples out there but saving time comes down to organization. Organizing your items at home, at work, in the garage, your backpack, and your files on your computer makes life easier because you don't have to waste time looking for items you need. Just think about the car keys, where are they? The keys are usually on the key hook by the entrance where most people put them. Take a look at your cell phone it's the same thing it's either in your pocket or its right on your night stand. Now imagine a time when you misplaced your keys and didn't put them on that key hook. Take a look at your cell phone it's the same thing once the phone ends up somewhere else because you didn't put it back you probably wasted time looking for it. There are simple tools that help you organize and if everything has a place you will never have to waste time doing tasks that waste time.

Save your time and properly organize your entire life. Everything has a place and everything can be organized. We don't think about things this way but organization will save you time and eliminate wasted time. Organization will save you more time so organize everything and stick to it.

Little Changes Big Difference

"If you are going to achieve excellence in big things, you develop the habit in little matters. Excellence is not an exception, it is a prevailing attitude." Charles R. Swindoll

Many of us think that making a big change will make a big difference. Sometimes this is true but some people that quit smoking cold turkey start up again after some time. People who incorporate small changes seem to quit for good or if they start something gradually they end up sticking to it. It may be difficult to start something that you have never done in your life and then keep doing it forever. Sometimes you have to build up to it and give yourself time to acclimate to whatever you are trying to do. There are people who go out to eat every day but aren't happy with the way they look. For them the best thing to do is to stop going out to eat at fast food restaurants and make healthy food at home. To someone that has never done that, it may seem like a huge problem and very inconvenient. Another way to handle this problem would be to start out slow and incorporate one home meal a week and keep doing it until you are comfortable with it. After time passes by, add one more day a week, spread them out if needed, and keep doing that until you are comfortable. After some time, give it a few months, even a year and you will prefer the homemade food instead of the restaurant. This can be applied to anything, let's say you smoke and you want to quit, reduce the cigarettes you smoke per day to one less than the day before or the week before or the month before. Time will pass and eventually you will quit smoking. I can go on forever about the little things that can be done that add up to a big difference but the point I made is here and it can be applied to anything. Make small changes and over time you will be rewarded with great results.

Challenge Everything

I love to challenge everything! It's one of my absolute favorite things to do. Now what I mean by this statement is really what it is saying, I want to challenge everything. I challenge myself to do better at everything and I always set higher goals. If we live a life that is constant we will never become better or do anything mentionable. If we try to challenge ourselves we can make extraordinary things happen. As a human race, we have accomplished so much and there are many more things we can accomplish. Things that seem simple now such as a radio, or a television didn't even exist a short time ago. Now we have planes, cars, rockets, and cell phones that can perform a million times faster than the first computers that were built and took up an entire room. We are all extraordinary and we can all think of new things, all we must do is challenge our minds and make ourselves better.

There are many times when I wake up and I think of a new goal or a challenge that I set out for myself. Sometimes I wake up and think of one thing such as an improvement to my job. I think of the changes and how I can make one thing better. When I arrive at work I set my mind to make this one thing better. As an example, I thought of a better way to track all of my customer issues so when I started working I made a note to myself to finish this one thing before the day is over. After many distractions, I was able to sit down and generate a spreadsheet that allowed me to track everything conveniently. I was able to set completion dates and ongoing notes for myself. I was so focused on this tool that I made for myself that I was able to eliminate customer issues much faster and keep track of my daily activities much more efficiently. This is just one example but there are many others that you can do for yourself.

Improve

Everything in the world needs improvement it doesn't matter how well you think everything is it can always be better and don't forget that. I have an industrial engineering background and if you are not familiar with industrial engineering it is about improving everything and that is my reason for writing this book. I started to work for an automotive company where the reporting for quality issues was required and consumed eight hours of my time every month. I saw the process as very tedious and boring, the reports were very useful and necessary, and we definitely needed them. I had to generate many quality charts then copy and paste them in presentations. By the second time I started generating the same reports I realized that there must be a better way to do this and there was. I researched better ways and found several processes that I could eliminate by using certain tables to generate the reports automatically. I saved over seven hours of my time for all of the reports. I did however spend over eight hours trying to find out how to do what I did. Now if you look at the time savings, I used eight hours to make it better and reduced the time to one hour instead of eight. By the next month I was able to save the time and start other time saving projects since I gained seven hours every month to do more.

No matter how good you think something is it can always be better. If you have a mindset such as this it will help you excel at everything you put your hands on. Don't just do the same thing repeatedly, be creative and try new things. Set the fear of failure a side and be positive. Set high standards and ensure that everything you improve is perfect or as close to perfect as possible. Just in case you are wondering if you do fail at improving something you will still feel better about yourself and if its work related your boss will be very happy with the initiative you took.

Be creative

In this section we will show you how to be creative. Being creative means many different things for everyone. For myself being creative is doing something different with the same technology or just improving it and making it better. Let me tell you about a few products that are out today such as a trash bag, it's made of plastic and it holds garbage but there are many new improvements that came along now. We have trash bags that are scented so your garbage doesn't stink. Another new development for the trash bag is the new force-flex bags that are using less plastic and have ridges in them so they can stretch more and avoid being torn. There are different thicknesses and sizes as well. As you can see there is a simple product that was made much better just because someone was creative. Being creative does not necessarily mean you have to invent new products or make new things it just means thinking outside of the box and improving or making things different.

How do you learn to be creative? The answer is... Many of us have difficulty of being creative and we are stuck being realistic and thinking like an adult. When you think like an adult you take into consideration of all the outcomes and possibilities of something that we know.

We do not think outside the box or we don't let ourselves be creative due to the fear of being judged.

To be more creative we have to let go of the fear of being judged and let ourselves imagine things that may not be normal. To be more creative you have to think like a kid. Kids are the most creative because they do not have the fear of failure or being judged. They are confident and they can say things that may not make sense. Thinking like a kid will help you come up with the wildest ideas. While some of the ideas may not be perfect others can and will be something that you can use. Don't be afraid to think like a kid and let go of the fear of being judged. In a brainstorming session, the rule is that no idea is wrong so put them all down.

CONCLUSION

Planning is the key to success. If you plan to get it done you will get it done. The key to planning is to do it and commit to it, to see it through until the end. When I started my book, I set my goal which was to write it. Then I gave myself a timeline to get it done as part of the goal. I specifically set a date to conduct research about writing the book. I set dates, times, and sometimes locations where I would work on this book. I went to the library so that I could focus, concentrate, and read books. I gave myself a time limit so I could stick to it concentrate and get it done. I used my calendar to schedule when and what I will do with specific timelines and goals.

As you can see if you are organized and plan it out with specifics, it helps you accomplish anything you want. If you want to become a football player just research, plan, practice, get everything that you have researched done and it will work out. If you want to lose weight research, plan, and get it done. It's as simple as one, two, and three. With a slogan such as this there is nothing that can't be done. Become a doctor research, plan, and get it done. Become an actor just research, plan, and get it done. Everything is truly that simple, so as long as you follow the proper steps you set out to do and ensure that you do them, then you will be able to accomplish everything you ever wanted and even have time to do more.

In this book, we went over three main topics Set, Plan, and Commit. In section titled "Set" We have learned how to find ourselves, what our needs are, and discover what we really need. This section allowed you to set the right goals which should lead you to ultimate happiness. The next section titled "Plan" we explored how to learn to accomplish that goal by properly planning. Now we should have a complete plan with assigned dates and actions in place to achieving our ultimate goals. As part of the last section titled "Commit" we found our motivation and created a reward system. We have also discovered ways to improve our lives by saving time, learning to be more creative, challenging ourselves to be better, and the commitment it takes to achieve your goals. Now we are half way to achieving our ultimate happiness goals. I hope you have learned much from this book and it has prepared you to properly set goals and accomplish them.

Thank you for reading my book ☺

Tadas Bite

Follow my Blog at NowYoureHappy.com ☺ to learn more about living happy

Like My page Now You're Happy on facebook.com/nowyourehappy/ for daily inspiration.

Tadas Bite is a first-generation Lithuanian. His parents brought him to the U.S. at the age of eleven. He was a kid who had to learn the English language and make new friends. He lived a normal life struggling in school and mostly being the class clown. He will be the first one to tell you that he has made more mistakes in his life than he can count. He has lived an interesting life thus far and he wants to share with you how he changed and what made him change for the better. He's not perfect but he has embraced many positive traits. Tadas wasn't always a positive person and a multitasking superstar as some of his friends have referred to him. He was just an average person with many various obstacles in the way of achieving success at being happy. Despite many obstacles he obtained his Bachelor's degree in Industrial Engineering and earned his Master's in Technology from Purdue University while working various odd jobs to pay for school and enjoying his hobby of bodybuilding. Currently he is working as an Engineer for a major medical device manufacturing company. At the same time, he is pursuing his dream to retire from his current profession and continue to work on the one true passion he has. Tadas wants to help the world become a happier place to live for everyone. His transformation started with setting goals and accomplishing them. Soon after he accomplished some of his goals his life transformed into something he has never dreamed of before. He has overcome many obstacles and worked very hard to get where he is now. He is so happy with the way his life has turned out and he is literally living in a happy dream now. He is so excited about sharing his story with you and how we can change to overcome anything and accomplish everything. He simply set goals, and accomplishes them and he wants to show you how, so you can end up being ultimately happy.

Tadas mission in life is to help everyone in the world become happier.

He wrote this book to show each reader how easy it really is to set your goals for ultimate happiness and achieve them.

Printed in the United States
By Bookmasters